WHAT
THE
FLY
HEARD

WHAT THE FLY HEARD:
What mediators say behind closed doors
Sandi Adams, MSCM

First Edition June 1998
Second Edition February 2002

Illustrations & cover design:
Lesley Johnson

The material in this manual has been written to assist beginning
mediators get a clearer picture of the work of the mediator so that
they may develop the very best practices. Permission will be
given for individual pages to be reproduced and shared provided
1) the ownership of S. Adams remains on the page, 2) no profit is
derived from its reproduction, and 3) S. Adams is informed of the
intended use.

To contact Sandi Adams, or for more information
about her trainings and workshops:

Sandi Adams
520 Princess Street
Wilmington, NC 28401
910-254-1284
sandia@wilmington.net

ISBN   0-9666525-0-9

About The Author

SANDI ADAMS, MSCM, has been providing mediation services, trainings, conflict resolution workshops and meeting services to individuals, agencies, academic institutions, and organizations since 1982. Her mediation work has included mediating a wide variety of interpersonal and multi-party disputes, facilitating staff retreats and difficult group discussions, training and mentoring new mediators, and serving as a mediator for the Department of Justice's Americans with Disabilities Act mediation project.

Prior to going into private practice in 1983, she was the Director of the Mediation Training Program at Woodbury College in Montpelier, Vermont. In addition to teaching and training while there, she also coordinated the small claims mediation project and the Dispute Resolution Center where she provided mediation, facilitation, and conflict resolution services for individuals and groups throughout the state. Previously, she held positions in Pennsylvania, Virginia and western New York. She has provided diverse types of workshops and trainings in conflict resolution and mediation to a variety of groups and has designed and implemented mediation programs in communities and schools.

Sandi has her Masters of Science in Conflict Management from George Mason University and has received numerous additional trainings in the field. She has served in officer positions on the boards of the Colorado Council of Mediators and Mediation Organization, the Vermont Mediators Association, and the Society of Professionals in Dispute Resolution New England chapter, and the National Conference on Peacemaking and Conflict Resolution. She is an associate editor of <u>Peacemaking in Your Neighborhood: Mediator's Handbook</u>, 2nd ed., has published articles in *Conciliation Quarterly*, *The Fourth R*, *Friends Journal*, and the *CCMO Monthly*.

About The Illustrator

LESLEY JOHNSON has been a published illustrator since 1992. Her B.S. in Forest Biology from the State University of New York College of Environmental Science and Forestry along with her creative and artistic abilities come together in illustrations of natural science subjects. Along with illustrating, she also runs lesleydesign.com, a Web site design business. Lesley resides in Louisville, Colorado.

Thanks & Appreciation

To numerous colleagues, students, and friends over the years, but especially to the following individuals for their special help in the publication of this book.

Lee Bryan and Alice Estey, Woodbury College
Lesley Johnson, lesley johnson illustrations
Debbie Jordan, Cottrell Printing
Bill Schwartz, Family Mediation Group

Table of Contents

OTHER BUSINESS:

THE BUZZ ABOUT IMPARTIALITY AND CONFIDENTIALITY

ON-GOING EDUCATION AND SKILL DEVELOPMENT

Introduction

"I would love to be a fly on the wall."

Humans, being of a curious nature, have developed sayings such as this to indicate their desire to know things or hear things that are not easily available to them. I have heard many a newly trained or beginning mediator ask to observe or listen to "a real mediation" so that they might get a better idea and understanding of what exactly the mediator does and says to assist parties in a session. "How do you learn mediator-speak?" they ask. Roleplays in training bring us only so close, and there is so much new information to juggle that it is natural to feel the desire to watch an experienced mediator work in a real case.

An opportunity to observe seasoned mediators is rare for many beginning mediators, however. It is my goal here to provide an additional alternative in this book. I will provide a variety of examples of "mediator-speak": what a mediator might say in each section of the mediation, in response to typical dilemmas and needs in a session, to do our work of supporting the parties, helping them negotiate, and attending to the process.

I hope this book of examples will be helpful to those seeking a clearer idea of how a mediator may actually work and respond when needed. The examples are drawn from a variety of types of conflicts and mediations. While I have given names to certain stages of a mediation, in models that vary from such stages, the examples should still fit for the objectives cited.

In each section, the examples will provide variations on wording, message, and objectives. It may be a solo mediator speaking, or a statement from a co-mediation team member. It is not the intent that the examples be taken as a whole, that a mediator has to say something in these exact ways, or that any statement may be used in all mediations.

In some sections you will see part of a statement in parenthesis and underlined. This information is provided to complete the example, but would change based on the content of a specific mediation and what the mediator was hearing or trying to check. Think of the underlined section as where you would fill in the blank.

Finally, this collection is not meant to replace training in any way. It is provided, in fact, as a follow-up to training and as a supplement to a training manual. The examples stand to provide modeling only. Training, manuals, and supervised experience are needed to understand the reasons behind certain language and statements, when they might be appropriate and useful, and how to decide when mediator intervention is needed at all.

STAGES
OF
MEDIATION

Listening In On The Mediator's Opening Statement

Here are some examples of what mediators may say to begin a mediation session where explaining mediation and setting the tone are the goals. This statement should be brief, concise, and appropriate to the situation. Remember, parties are often nervous and/or anxious to begin and may not be taking in all that you are saying.

Thank you for being willing to give mediation a try.

We're going to ask each of you, one at a time, to take a minute to tell us what's brought you here, and then there will be an opportunity to respond or ask questions. During this initial time we'd ask that the speaker not be interrupted and we will not be asking questions either.

This is an opportunity for the two of you to have a different type of conversation than you may have had before. My job is to help you have the conversation in a productive way. I am not here to give advice, decide who may be right or wrong, or to tell anyone what to do.

While waiting your turn to speak during the beginning time, you may want to write down anything you hear that is new or different, or that raises questions for you. After each of you have spoken, these may be some of the things you want to follow-up on.

You will see us taking notes. They are to help us follow the information you are sharing. We will not be keeping these notes when the mediation is over.

Are there any questions before we begin?

To begin, I'm going to ask that each of you speak one-at-a-time and tell me what the trouble has been between you. You will each have a turn and then there will be a chance for you to respond to what you have heard from each other. Is this something you can each agree to do?

It can be helpful in mediation for us to speak with each of you separately. If we ask for time to do this, or if you'd like a chance to speak with us privately, all that is said there will be kept confidential.

We believe that mediation is voluntary. Are you both here willing to participate in the discussion?

As far as I am concerned, everything you say is confidential; I will not be reporting your conversation to anyone.

Just to remind you, as mediators we are not advocates or judges. We are here to assist in guiding your conversation so that it might be as productive as possible for you and help you understand what is important to each of you.

Sometimes it is helpful to meet separately with each of you. If we ask for such a meeting, please be assured that what might be said privately we will not be repeating or sharing without your explicit request to do so.

Would either of you ask anything else of us or each other before we begin?

If you need a break for any reason, please let us know. Bathrooms and a water fountain are located down the hall to the right. Coffee is available in the lounge. We'd request that smoking breaks be taken outside as this building does not permit smoking inside.

Is there anything that you've heard or not heard that would keep you from wanting to proceed?

Are you willing to move ahead, then?

Bill, would you be willing to go first? *(answering 'yes')*
Is that o.k. with you, Rob?

Which of you would be willing to begin? *(offer)*
Is that o.k. with you, Jay? *(discussion)*
O.k. Jill, it seems that you both agree you can begin.

In these situations I usually begin with the person who made the initial contact. That would be you, Jan. Are you willing to start? *(answering 'yes')*
Is that o.k. with you Mark?

Things Mediators Say To Clarify Information And Parties' Interests

This is the time when we want to move parties into dialogue with each other rather than towards us. Now, mediators want to: draw out more information; clarify everybody's understanding and perspectives; help them hear each other's perspectives; listen for, check out, and reflect interests; reflect new understandings, feelings, and common concerns; listen for issues for discussion and potential negotiation.

You had wanted to respond to each other and I had asked you to wait. Thank you for waiting and please feel free to speak with each other now. I also have some questions to understand the situation better.

Tell me more about what happened when <u>(you couldn't get your car out of the driveway)</u>?

How did you discover that was a problem for her?

What happens when <u>(you need to study but they are at home)</u>?

Say more about <u>(the supply area and how it works)</u>.

You are really concerned with <u>(how the agency can be the best it can)</u>.

Both of you sound really frustrated with <u>(how others have been talking about you)</u>.

Is part of the problem for you that (you can't get get ready for work on time, and now you're worried how this will impact your work performance)?

It seems that (safety in the common driveway) is important to each of you. Is that right?

You've said that (it's been hard to talk with him about your ideas for Amanda) but it sounds like (you'd like to to include him, have conversations with him about your daughter if it were easier). Am I understanding that right?

Could you say more about how that's a problem for you?

Were you aware of that?

How long have you (been working with each other)?

And when did tensions begin to rise about (project deadlines)?

What changed from when you (first moved in together and you say it was fine to the fight that happened last month)?

How long has (phone usage caused a problem between you)?

Did what she just said come as a surprise to you?

Is that new information for you?

How do you see (your time in the apartment)?

(Being treated in a way that feels like respect) is important to you, as is (having the information you need to get the work done). Is that right?

(It's been really hard for you these past few months and having a sense that this is moving forward) seems important to you, Quinline.

Flies In The Ointment -
Sticky Comments To Avoid

DURING MEDIATOR'S OPENING STATEMENT you want to be sure that your words are clear and brief without making pat statements or guarantees. Your hope is to put them more at ease, not raise their anxieties or feed into any feelings of "this is hopeless." Comments to AVOID:

Mediation is an opportunity for you to make agreements on how to solve your problem.

This session is confidential. No one will talk about it outside this room.

Are you here by your own volition?

We will come to agreements and write them down for you.

I might want to meet with one of you alone and I won't tell the other what you have said.

We're going to control how you talk about your problem.

If you don't solve it here you might end up in court and a judge will decide.

We're going to facilitate this process and assist you in seeking a resolution.

You have to tell the truth and you have to be respectful of each other or we will end the mediation.

WHEN GATHERING INFORMATION & INTERESTS watch out for your jargon and repeating any loaded language or slanted views that one party may have. Steer clear of cross-examining in your questions, talking about parties' initial positions, trying to analyze, or getting "the facts." And remember, this is NOT the time to look for solutions. Comments to AVOID:

So, you have a problem with her (<u>harassment and you don't like how catty she is</u>), right?

Tell us what your problem is.

So, what are your interests?

Why do you do that to her?

Exactly when did that happen? Are you sure?

Is that true?

What is it you want him to do?

So, you want (<u>$50 for the broken saw</u>) and you (<u>don't want to give it to him</u>).

What's the *real* problem here?

Do you agree that (<u>you harass her</u>)?

Do you think that's really true?

Is it that you are jealous of him?

Are you messy at home?

So, you want (<u>Jillian every weekend</u>) and you want (<u>Jillian with you at least every other weekend</u>).

So who (<u>stopped talking to who</u>) first?

How often do you (<u>space out and forget to update the appointment book</u>)?

So, how can you be (<u>less controlling</u>) in this situation?

Why haven't you been more neighborly?

Is it that you feel she tries to control you?

Eavesdropping On Issue Checklist And Agenda Setting

After it is felt that all the information has been clarified and understood, and AFTER the mediators know the interests of ALL parties, it is time to frame the issues and set an agenda for discussing those issues. The goal here is to have the parties "buy-in" to the issue list. That is, finding problem frames that: feel right for all parties, do not favor anyone or suggest one person's perspective of a problem, do not suggest solutions, and that all parties feel would be useful to talk about.

Lead ins:

Let me check and see if I've understood what you could talk about here. . .

So, the items that need to be discussed are . . .

Do I understand that . . . are the issues you'd like to see resolved?

Sampling of issue/problem frames:

The landing and what might be kept there, and how it will be kept.

How you can both get your computer work done.

Where to store outside play equipment.

How you're going to speak with each other when problems arise.

How to get the chores done so you each feel it's fair.

Noise, particularly stereo and t.v. noise, and times of day they are a problem for each of you.

Speaking to board members, particularly about what items and in what manner.

Use of the common driveway.

How to plan projects together.

What will happen when one of you is not available for the other to consult with.

Sarah's piano lessons, particularly how they will be paid for and her transportation to lessons.

To check for accuracy & buy-in, you might say:

Do you feel these are all your concerns?

Did I miss anything?

Have I understood?

Are these the issues you'd like to talk about?

Are these correct?

Anything else?

What did I miss?

The agenda:

I suggest you begin with (<u>use of the computer</u>) as you both have some urgent concerns around this. How does that sound to you?

Because it's central to all the other concerns, I'd suggest you talk about (<u>what you each need to complete the current project</u>), then (<u>division of upcoming project tasks, how to communicate with each other about joint project work</u>), and then, (<u>what you will communicate to your boss about the project and this mediation</u>). Does this sound right to both of you?

You might want to begin with (<u>issues around Sarah's piano lessons</u>), then come back to (<u>the car insurance payments and how you can each share in celebrating Sarah's birthday</u>). Would this make sense to you as a way to continue?

If these are the three issue that you'd like to address, does any one jump out to you as the place to start?

Mediator-Speak During The Negotiation Stage

Assisting your parties to negotiate effectively involves continued keen listening, good judgment on when to intervene and when not to, and a large array of tools for intervening. Clarifying interests, summarizing new understandings, checking for points of agreement, drawing out all ideas, exploring the alternatives and their consequences, patience, and encouragement are all important ways to stay focused on <u>our</u> role while allowing the parties to do <u>their</u> work.

What (<u>chores</u>) do you each believe (<u>need to get done</u>)?

How would you know (<u>if it were "fair"</u>)?

If you feel (<u>storing them would work</u>), then what possibilities are there for (<u>storing them</u>)?

How would that work?

What other ideas do you have?

You said that (<u>contacting volunteers sometimes</u>) would be o.k. with you. What (<u>times in particular</u>) would be o.k.?

Would that resolve (<u>the problem of feeling safe in the yard</u>) for you?

You've both indicated an interest in (<u>continuing the business</u>). Now you need to work out specifics around (<u>how and when to accept jobs and how to communicate potential jobs to each other</u>). So, (<u>the phone rings and someone's asking for your services</u>). What do you want to have happen next?

What do you want (<u>Jamie</u>) to know about how that is important to you?

How does that work for you over a period of time?

What happens then?
What problems does that pose or create?

How do you want him to (<u>come to you if he would like to stay late</u>)?

You said, Joe, (<u>that you'd prefer not to speak with Phil about the meeting agenda</u>). How does this work to your benefit?

Is your idea possible given (<u>your work roles and responsibilities</u>)?

Are you saying that (<u>some things on the landing</u>) are o.k? *(answering 'yes')* What things are you thinking would be o.k.?

That's the first time you've indicated a (<u>possibility in paying for some of the car insurance</u>). Say more about that.

What have you tried so far (<u>around sharing the computer</u>)?

You've already agreed to (<u>finish the current project and to update each other on your parts each week directly after the 9 a.m. meeting</u>). And you've talked about (<u>your different styles of work to help each other understand and see that you are both dedicated to the project being a success</u>). What are you going to do if, for example, (<u>the other isn't as far along as you believe the task should be, or if something isn't as detailed</u>)?

If you can't resolve (<u>how the bill gets paid</u>), what will happen?

What doesn't work about (how you share the food costs now)?

Is that an idea you would like to talk more about?

If it were working well, what would be different?

What do you need her to do so you (don't lose your morning time)?

It sounds like you both agree (Friday mornings work as private time for Katie).

How does that help (you feel your girls will be safe when they are walking home), which you said was very important to you?

What do you think about what he's just said?

When would you (replace it)?

How will it (be paid for)?

What happens if this doesn't work on the schedule you've agreed to so far?

You both agree that (efficiency in the meetings is important). What do you each want to do to (make them efficient)?

You've already agreed that you'll (each pay some part of the costs). What would you propose as (your part)?

You each indicated (supervision of the workers during the day) would be o.k. Micky, what would (supervision) look like to you? *(response)* Janet, what do you mean by (supervision)?

You Could Get Burnt –
Don't Fly Near These

DURING ISSUE CHECKLIST AND AGENDA SETTING you want to work diligently to keep from identifying issues in ways that suggest solutions, label a problem as belonging to one person or another, or letting your judgments creep in. If problems aren't framed in a way that parties can negotiate around what needs to be resolved for the future, it will not be helpful either. AVOID:

So, you two need to divide up the chores evenly.

Your problem, Walt, is keeping Julia through Sunday night. And, Carol, your problem is that Walt doesn't give you enough lead-time on schedule changes he wants.

The issue you need to resolve is where Jane can put her money so Helen doesn't get accused of taking it.

You need to figure out how to work with each other given that you are so different.

The problem is that Gene isn't spending enough time with Pat.

The problem is that you need to communicate better.

You have a personality conflict.

You have a problem with Kyle's silence and Kyle has a problem with your needing to talk about every little thing.

The problem is that you two haven't paid the rent for 2 months.

DURING THE NEGOTIATION STAGE be clear that it is not your job to solve anyone's conflict. Again, your opinions, biases, judgments, and ideas need to be kept in check. Also, stay away from statements that push for agreements, push one party's suggestion, or that show impatience with the negotiations. Remember, if they don't make any agreements it's o.k. Mediation isn't just about making agreements - it's an opportunity to talk, to be heard, and to discover any new understandings. Also, be sure everyone is clear which issue they are talking about - being too general or vague can feel confusing or discouraging to parties. **AVOID:**

How can she get to the computer when she wants to?

Can't you do that?

What you two need to do is to divide the work load.

How do you want to solve this?

That sounds good.

Is this really that important?

If you agree to replace it, you'll do that by when? Next week?

Kelly's idea was good. Don't you want to talk about it some more?

Why can't you do that? He said he's going to pay half like you asked for.

Could you be more respectful to him in the future?

Somebody has to take Eliza to the rink each morning; why not just alternate mornings?

You've agreed on what to do about almost all the chores. How about you split the remaining few?

Don't you want to solve this problem?

This is really getting nowhere.

This isn't working.

Hannah says she only needs you to be available between 3 and 5 in the afternoon. Why can't you do that?

If you're concerned about how he's talking with customers on the phone, maybe you should get one of those monitoring devices that customer service departments use.

You want to be a good parent don't you? How about seeing your daughter more than once a month? Most couples do every other weekend.

Say What? Finalizing Any Agreements And Agreement Writing

After discussion of the issues and any negotiating, mediators may need to assist parties to finalize any points of agreement and/or next steps. Statements of principle and shared points of view are reiterated or summarized. Help them and their agreements be specific, positive, and balanced. Check that they have provided for the future.

Phil agrees to (<u>invite all 12 staff members to staff meetings which will be scheduled the first Monday of each month</u>). Joe agrees to (<u>attend all staff meetings</u>). And with these agreements, you both said you believe (<u>your concerns about communications in the office would be addressed</u>). Great, and you both seem committed to making it work. So, what happens, say, when (<u>one of you will need to be away, is sick, or otherwise unable to attend a particular staff meeting</u>)?

You've both agreed that (<u>David will check with Sam before signing any paperwork</u>). Do you need to talk about anything else around how this will happen? When (<u>you'll check or what will be said</u>), for example?

You've made some tentative agreements throughout the discussion. Let's go back over everything and review so you can consider if the things you've each said you could do still feel o.k. If they do, I'll write those points down for you each to have a copy.

You've each had some new insights and understandings about the (<u>tensions that were occurring between you</u>). Having heard these, is there anything more you want to say?

Sally agrees to (<u>smoke only when Earl's not at her house</u>). Earl agrees to (<u>call first before coming over for a visit</u>). You both feel these steps will (<u>stop the arguing about smoking at Sally's house</u>). Do you need to talk about (<u>other locations, events, or time together</u>) when this may be an issue?

(<u>Melissa's adjustment to her new school</u>) is very important to each of you, clearly. And you both agree that (<u>you want to do all that you can to support her and help her, especially in not having her feel like she will lose all her old friends</u>). Given that, in what ways do you (<u>want to help her not feel that way</u>)?

There are 20 minutes left in our scheduled time. You've made several agreements with each other. I suggest the remaining time be used to check them and finalize any parts that may need it. Would that be helpful to you?

These points cover all the items you raised. Is there anything else that you can think of before we begin to wrap-up ?

Closing Statement Statements

Whether the meeting is ending with everybody in agreement, or if it is ending with the knowledge that parties are now moving on to other steps for resolution to their concerns, provide a clear end to the meeting. Acknowledge what has been accomplished as honestly yet positively as possible. Let them know the good work they did without gushing or insincerity.

You've both worked very hard in talking about (the situation in your apartment building). It wasn't easy, but you have each indicated a different understanding than when you came in.

Thank you for your willingness to come today and talk about your concerns. You have each indicated your next steps at this point to try to (resolve the bill in dispute). Good luck to both of you.

Well, you are clearly in a different place than when you came here! Congratulations on all your hard work. You really listened to each other and found ways to understand how each of your actions had actually hurt the other person. Recognizing this made finding answers to some of the problems much easier. Good for you.

Great work, Jim and Carl. At this point, barring any final comments either of you would like to make, the session is over.

While you're signing the agreements you've made, do you have any comments or feedback for us about your experience in mediation?

Good luck to both of you. I hope things will be easier for you now.

Well, you have each heard some difficult things and there remains some uncertainty about how things are going to be in the future. We want to wish you both the best in your next steps. If you feel that mediation would be useful again in the future, please give the Dispute Center a call.

Having reviewed the points you've covered so far, it seems that this forum is helping you move forward. Would you like to meet again to work on the issues you didn't have an opportunity to discuss today?

Flypaper -
Don't Get Caught In These Traps

DURING FINALIZING ANY AGREEMENTS AND AGREEMENT WRITING don't get caught in pushing for solutions or making assumptions. Don't be afraid to raise questions that may change or void parts of tentative agreements. Good agreements are specific, not vague. **AVOID:**

So, you're going to make sure that Bella gets to class on time, because that's important. And you should call if something comes up, right?

Louis, you said earlier that you'd bring Athena to her after-school events. It would have to be o.k., then, if Shirleen does the weekend activities, right?

You're time's almost up. Can't you agree on something?

If you don't decide what to do about the bill, you'll both end up with a bad credit rating and probably will have to go to small claims court.

So, Fran promises not to hang up when Lisa calls and Lisa will be polite, too.

You both agree not to talk to each again.

Greg agrees he'll fix his fence and Alex promises not yell at him again.

DURING CLOSING STATEMENTS watch out for under or over stating the reality of the meeting. Also be careful not to show any frustration with them, or make them feel as if they failed. **AVOID:**

Your time is up so you can go now.

Too bad you couldn't come to any agreements.

You did a fantastic job! I just can't believe how wonderful this has turned out considering how awful it was when you started!

Well, we all did the best we could and you have something even though it's not what you wanted.

Wow, you have really worked hard. You have both done excellent work; you've come so far together. I just know that you will be able to work this out before too long and that everything will be o.k. between you someday.

OTHER
BUSINESS

Checking For Understanding
And Gathering Information

A key element in the mediator's work is to be sure that both you as mediator and the parties understand accurately what each party is saying and what is important to them. Paraphrasing, asking elicitive questions, summarizing, restating, acknowledging and encouraging are all tools that are used for information gathering and checking for understanding.

So, you believe this has (been most upsetting) for you because of (the time you are losing), is that right?

Can you tell me more about how you view the (scheduling of events)?

It sounds like you have been struggling with this for quite a while and you're feeling (pretty tired from it).

Is (having clear communication about the dates and times of each report) what is important to you?

What happened (in the last meeting that upset you)?

What concerns you about how (he responds to Amanda)?

When did that happen?

How does (having her there) affect you?

Do I understand correctly that you're concerned about (your daughter's safety when she walks home from Brad's house)?

You've both said many difficult things that have shed new light on the situation for each of you. Perhaps now can look at how you might want to move forward differently than you had before.

You're having a really strong reaction to what he just said. Are you o.k.?

Clearly you both (want to be involved with how the products are marketed and you care about how your work is seen within the company).

Clara, you're reluctant to (pay for the tree damage because you don't believe it is your fault). Is that right?

What's the most important thing you want Martin to understand?

You're frustrated because you believe (you've made repeated attempts to speak with Teal about this and haven't gotten any response)?

Tell us more about what happened (during the three months of the project).

More Issue Framing
& Breaking Them Into Specifics

Again, before moving into any negotiating, it is vital to frame (another word for state) the issues, or problems, in a way that the parties feel captures the concerns they need to address. An issue needs to be framed in a way that it:
- □　　　favors no one
- □　　　does not contain any solution
- □　　　uses neutral language
- □　　　presents problem as shared by both
- □　　　states the problem to be resolved.

Well formed issue frames can often be broken down into specific pieces for negotiation. Breaking issues into such specifics aids people in being able to consider potential ideas for resolution.

Situation: Roommates at odds with each other when one's new sweetheart enters the picture. Problems arise about having "alone" time and being able to feel comfortable in the apartment. Accusations of sloppiness and nagging are exchanged as well as who's paying for and who's eating what food.

Sample frame:
- How the apartment is shared so you both feel it's comfortable and fair.
- Specifically, how to assure time in the apartment without being interrupted by others; how much time BJ will be at the apartment; and what activities you each consider for the living room and what for the bedroom.
- How to speak with each other when problems arise.
- Household chores. Specifically, what needs to be done, how to get it done, and how to assess if it's done in a way that is acceptable to both of you.
- How food purchasing and preparation will work.

Situation: Neighbors have been arguing over dogs in the trash, cars in the driveway and on the street, and each other's kids' foul language and back talk. Fights have broken out between the kids in the past, and recently between two of the parents.

Sample frame:
- How to assure trash can be safely put out for pick up.
- What cars are to be parked where.
- How to talk with each other when problems occur, specifically, problems between the kids & problems with any other issues between the two households.
- Children's behavior to the other's family members.

Imagine how you might frame each of the following scenarios. After you've thought of several, turn the page to see some possible examples.

1.) Arguing sweethearts:

A.J. - "You're rigid and uptight; I always have to do what you say. There's no spontaneity."

B.J. - "You're rude and inconsiderate; you're always changing plans at the last minute. It happens all the time. Be more responsible!"

2.) Landlord & Tenant:

Tenant - "Stop telling other tenants and my friends that I'm trash. If you have a problem with me, tell me. You're always coming around to spy on me and my friends. Why don't you spend your time taking care of your responsibilities like fixing the garbage disposal."

Landlord - "I can't talk to you; you always ignore me and just go back to your partying. It's not required I provide you with a new disposal - read your lease. And *you* stop talking about *me* behind my back!"

3.) Lila's separated parents:

Mom - "You have no idea how to handle Lila when she is having a temper tantrum or refuses to go to bed. You're spoiling her and you make the situation worse."

Dad - "What makes you think you know what's right?! You're the one who makes her scream with your need to control everything and everybody."

4.) Americans with Disabilities Act Grievance:

ADA Complainant - "You're breaking the law. There's not enough accessible parking and the spaces you do have are always used by delivery vans coming to your store. And when I want to leave the store, it requires an employee to help me through the 'enter' door, which is the only one wide enough for my chair - and they are never around to help!"

Respondent - "Those three spaces are always empty; there's no need to make more. I've got an accessible process in place, you just don't like it and are harassing me."

Examples of potential frames:

1.) Arguing sweethearts:

How to make plans and discuss any changes in plans. OR
How to discuss potential changes in plans.   OR
Expectations for making and changing plans.   OR
Spending time together and talking about your plans for time together.

2.) Landlord & Tenant:

Acceptable behaviors in the house.
Communication between the two of you and with others. Specifically how to approach and respond to each other, about what and when, and what's o.k. to say to others.
Expectations around the broken garbage disposal.

3.) Lila's separated parents:

How to respond when Lila misbehaves.   OR
Handling Lila's undesirable behaviors.   OR
Making decisions about how to react when Lila is upset.

4.) Americans with Disabilities Act Grievance:

How to assure accessible entry and egress at the store.   OR
Expectations of accessibility for the store.   OR
How to assess compliance with the law.

More Samples of Issue Frames:

The care and housing of Tabby, the cat.

What it would take for work on the roof to continue. Also, if work continues, how to interact and communicate with each other during the work day, and how the site will be left at the end of the work day.

The issue of homework, specifically, expectations on its quality, times it is to be done, and where to work on it.

Noise between your two houses, particularly car noise at night and dogs in the morning.

What's going to happen with the damage deposit.

Checking If Parties Have Needed Information & Giving Information

People do their best negotiating when they have all the information they need: information to understand the situation and information about potential options for resolution. As mediators, we have an obligation to check that our parties are fully informed for the work they are doing. Some of this work can be done with, or in the presence of, all parties. Sometimes it is best to inquire or inform parties in separate meetings.

What do each of you know about what happens when you go to court in cases like this?

Do either of you have any information about (landlord-tenant rights and responsibilities in your city)?

Where did you hear (that if you don't agree to pay that portion you'd be forced to)? Is that something you need to double check?

I'm not sure if that's an accurate understanding of how that policy would be carried out. How can you find out how it would be carried out in this situation?

What do you know about what Marc is saying?

In similar situations people have found (counseling) helpful. Would you be interested in information about this type of resource?

How can you get information that you trust about that?

What resources do you know of that are available to you?

I want to be sure you aren't making a decision based on incorrect information. Do you know of (an accountant) you could speak with?

I have a list of some professionals in this area that help people with this type of thing if you need it.

Do you know of anyone else who had to go through that process? What happened in their situation?

It doesn't sound like you both are working with the same breadth or depth of information about (the policies and procedures) that impact your situation. I'm going to suggest we spend a couple of minutes exploring how Antonia might get some information and then reschedule for another time.

Separate Meetings

Separate meetings, or caucuses, are often a useful tool for speaking with parties about unhelpful negotiating behaviors, to uncover hidden interests, to cool off parties, provide space for the shy speaker, help people explore what they want, or for meeting/strategizing with a co-mediator. Be clear whom you want to meet with first and where others are to wait. Meet with each party, even if your main piece of business is primarily with one. In the meeting, stay focused and when you reassure them of the meeting's confidentiality, be sure to honor it!

George, I've asked to meet separately with you because (you've been reluctant to speak in the session with Karl). Tell me more about what's going on for you.

Thanks for waiting, Joan. I want to take just a few minutes to speak with you about what ideas you have if (Kimberly and you are not able to figure out how to divide all the electronic equipment). What do you think will happen?

I can see that talking with Jameel about (the car) is really difficult for you. I wanted to just give you some time to speak with me in confidence about how this is going for you.

Blair, as you and Claudia have been talking (about the issues around the house you share), she's made several suggestions about how to resolve some of the problems. You haven't found any satisfactory, yet you haven't offered any ideas of your own. Can you tell me what's getting in the way for you?

...So, if you don't want to tell (Claudia that you really want to move out and she thinks you're here to negotiate those items we've listed about sharing the house), what do you want to talk about when we go back into the session with her?

We want to meet with each of you separately at this time and we'll meet with Harlan first, and then you, Vince. Just as a reminder, whatever is said privately we will not be sharing with the other or bringing back to the table ourselves.

Vince, let me show you where you can wait. If it's going to be more than a few minutes, I'll come and let you know.

Carol, clearly this is a difficult time in your life, and mediation isn't going to be able to help you with all the issues you are facing. While you and Burt will be able to talk about (what to do around the house issues and cars), I'm not sure that it's going to make you feel better regarding your work situation and the other stresses you've mentioned. Some people facing similar problems have found talking things through with a good counselor helpful. Would this be a resource you'd be interested in?

(to co-mediator): Linda, I'm thinking this might be a good time for us to meet and then possibly meet separately with Pat and Rita. What do you think?
(responding): I have just a couple more questions to follow up on what Rita was saying, and then I think it would be a good time for us to check in. *(to parties):* I can imagine that you two might like a little break as well.

How would you like that information to come up in the session?

What would you need to have happen so you wouldn't feel (like you had to keep interrupting her)?

I'm not sure I'm clear yet on (how the meetings are a problem for you). Could you explain to me privately why (you haven't been going)?

So, we're going to take a few minutes to meet with Robin now, and then when we're all back together I'll ask you what ideas you have (about the check book). Is that what we've agreed?

Separate Meeting NO-NOs

AVOID statements such as:

I'd like to take you aside and speak with you.

OR

I've taken you aside to tell you we're not going to continue if you keep breaking the rules by calling her names.

> *(Meeting separately should not feel like a reprimand or punishment to parties.)*

Gee, that Fred is really a pain. I can see why it's been so tough for you.

> *(It is not a time to side or bond with one party. Still retain your impartiality.)*

I wanted to meet with you to see if you'd tell me what's REALLY going on here.

OR

Certainly you can't be that mad because of the cat. What's the REAL reason you're mad at Cyndee?

> *(If you have a specific question or concern about unspoken information ask them, but be cautious of implying that they haven't been honest, or that what they have been talking about isn't important or a 'real' problem.)*

Non-Negotiable Issues

In mediation, people talk about many things that are bothering them or that have lead to their bringing their dispute to mediation. While these things can be discussed in a mediation, some are not "negotiable". Let parties know what is and isn't negotiable, identify the parts of issues that are negotiable, and help parties figure out what to do with those that are not.

You will never know (<u>who ran up the electricity bill, but now that you owe $200</u>), you can talk about (<u>what you want to do with that bill and how to assure it will not happen in the future</u>).

If Sarah is the only person who has the authority to make that decision and she isn't here, what can the two of you decide to do about (<u>your roles in the project</u>)?

It doesn't sound like you are going to be able to convince each other to believe or feel differently. Given that, what behaviors do you need to talk about to assure that (<u>you won't end up at the police station again</u>)?

You aren't going to be able to promise that you won't feel (<u>hurt if he fails to call you after saying he would</u>). Instead, what can you each expect if this happens?

If it's important to both of you (<u>what Ronny wants</u>), perhaps we need to put this issue aside for now until you can get that information. How do you want to get (<u>Ronny's input in this decision</u>)?

You will probably not agree whether (<u>Chris acted 'responsibly' or not</u>). But you can talk about what you would want to see each other do next time.

Clearly you both believe (<u>the girls should not be giving any of their lunch to Angel and Fluffy through the fence</u>), but since they are not here to make that agreement, what can either of you do to address this desire?

Whether (<u>Frank's sexist or not</u>) will probably not be proven or refuted here today. Is there anything you want to ask him to do, Monica, when working with you in the office?

Using Neutral Language

Another key piece of work that mediators do is to translate many of the slanted, loaded statements that parties make into statements that have less sting or zing. This often helps the other party to hear the concern as well. Along with framing issues neutrally, we must restate their words when they are biased in favor of one party's perspective. Here are some examples of slanted accusations and how a mediator might reframe the statement using neutral language.

She keeps her room like a filthy pig!

How she keeps her room is a concern.

You're rude and unprofessional and I will not cover for you with angry customers!

You're concerned about how customers are responded to.

You are nothing but a lying, cheating, s.o.b. that I could never trust to keep any agreement!

You need a greater sense that Tim will follow through with the agreements he's making.

She's into everybody's business and is totally controlling.

Gina's interaction with you is a problem.

You are so naive; you have no idea how this house has been managed and you'll just screw it up.

> *Making sure the household continues*
> *to be managed well is important to you.*

She is totally inconsiderate with coming in late, leaving early, and taking extra long lunches. Who does she think is doing all her work? Please!

> *You need her to know the impact that*
> *her actions have on your workload.*

THE
BUZZ
ABOUT
IMPARTIALITY
AND
CONFIDENTIALITY

The Buzz About Impartiality And Confidentiality

There are usually quite a number of questions in training about *how* to actually remain impartial and *what*, exactly, is confidential in a mediation. Let's take these one at a time.

REMAINING IMPARTIAL

Every one of us comes into mediation with all of our experiences, beliefs, values, and biases. We are not a blank slate by any means. To pretend to be so can keep us from reflecting on what of our experiences, beliefs, values and biases will get in the way of doing our work as "impartials". To ACT impartially means we had better be aware of what it is about OUR SELF that will get in the way of helping parties do what they need to do. If you are having a reaction to one of the parties, take a moment to figure out what it is and how YOU are going to deal with it. This one isn't their problem, it's yours. And don't fool yourself: if it's big enough, you will lose all your tools and will not be able to serve your parties.

Acting impartially means, in part:
◇ hearing and understanding <u>all</u> parties' interests
◇ allowing all parties to speak for themselves
◇ keeping yourself out of their content
◇ not buying into one party's side of the story
◇ not pushing one person's solutions or your own
◇ not assuming how you view something is how others view it

If you hear yourself or a co-mediator saying anything close to what follows, stop and check-in to assess if you have lost your ability to behave impartially.

x What Kelly is saying is . . .

x Kelly has a good idea here. Why don't you consider it, Stan?

x Let's see if we can't find a way for you to have the apartment to yourself at least a few days a week, Bryan.

x You said you want to be fair, Ty, so why not agree to split the bill with Jason?

x Have you considered paying her $50 per month until the full amount is paid?

x I don't understand how you can say that.

x That doesn't sound like a very fair offer.

x Can't you offer to do more than that?

INSTEAD:

✓ Stan, are you understanding Kelly's perspective on that?

✓ How do you respond to Kelly's idea, Stan?
    What ideas do you have?

✓ You said it's important for you to have private time in the apartment. How might you achieve that, Bryan?

✓ You said you want to be fair, Ty. What might fairness look like for you regarding payment of the bill?

✓ What ideas do you have for payment of the $350?

✓ Say more about how you're thinking that would work for your situation.

✓ That's one idea. What others might be possible?

✓ Will these ideas satisfy your need for privacy, Ryan, which you said was important?

CONFIDENTIALITY

What exactly is confidential in mediation? Are mediators required to report? What if someone talks about something illegal? These are common questions for beginning mediators. Let's look at each question.

WHAT IS CONFIDENTIAL IN MEDIATION?

If you tell parties that you will not be sharing what they say with anyone, you are committing to keep the information private. You are not promising or committing that they will not tell others about what was said. You can only speak for yourself and that it is not your role to report what they said or what they agreed to. In some programs mediators do let the referring agency know whether parties came to a mediation or if it was not appropriate for mediation.

Some programs have adopted a policy where mediators report certain information to a program administrator. In these programs, the mediator would inform the parties up front what they may need to disclose. An example of the opening statement might include:

As far as I'm concerned, I will not be sharing what you say here today with anyone and the notes I take are to help me keep track of the conversation. I will tear them up at the end of the mediation. However, if I hear the threat of any bodily harm to any person I am obligated to let the program supervisor know.

ARE MEDIATORS REQUIRED TO REPORT?

In most states, mediators are not "required reporters," a term used to distinguish those professionals who are required by law to report any incidence of abuse, neglect, or intent to harm. Check your state's code to see if mediators are required reporters. Each individual mediator should decide if they choose to report such matters. If so, inform parties as part of your opening statement.

WHAT IF SOMEONE TALKS ABOUT SOMETHING ILLEGAL?

A rare situation at best, but this is where your pre-mediating self-reflection is key. You will have to take stock in advance of mediating where you draw lines and what you will do if you hear of illegal activity. For some, there is a difference between a mention of drugs, of suicide, of adultery, of a gun, and of speeding. All could be illegal activities, but we may think of them differently. You may simply ask people not to speak of the offense further, or you may want to engage in a conversation with the party or parties about your discomfort. You may find yourself negotiating with them about what might happen next, including what your next steps might be.

ON-GOING
EDUCATION
AND
SKILL
DEVELOPMENT

On-Going Education And Skill Improvement

Nothing can replace training, nothing can replace actual experience, and nothing can replace on-going education. Training is only the beginning of a career-long learning process. And while it may be challenging to secure actual experience in many parts of the country, on-going education for improving skills and keeping skills sharp can be found in all regions of the United States.

On-going education opportunities are available in many forms: workshops and short trainings, conferences, peer reviews, apprenticeships and mentors, and journal articles and books. No matter what stage or year of mediation work one is in, on-going education needs to be made part of one's plan for improved practice. Keep track of your training and on-going education. There is the possibility that verification mediation education will be required to work in some arenas or it may be part of a certification process.

Connecting with both your local or regional mediation association as well as national organizations can provide valuable information about on-going educational opportunities. The networking opportunity these associations offer can not be underestimated, as well. For those interested in becoming involved with mediation professionally, these connections will be critical. I've included some resources here to assist you in making these connections.

Here's wishing you growing passion for the work of mediation. Remain steadfast and faithful to its principles of supporting and empowering the parties, leaving their fate in their hands, and allowing them to consider all options, including not reaching agreement. Continue to reflect on your work and develop greater understandings of your skills and how to use them. If you are able to do these things, then the service you provide your community will be powerful and respected, and will be a service that has the potential for greatly impacting conflict and how it is handled in your community.

In conclusion, whenever in doubt you can regularly fall back on these three all-encompassing mediator 'rules':

BE YOURSELF
BE HONEST
USE COMMON SENSE

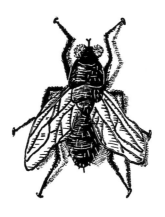

Best wishes.

NATIONAL MEMBERSHIP ORGANIZATIONS

There are a number of national organizations that provide invaluable information and networking opportunities. Each of the organizations listed holds at least one national conference a year. Conferences are a wonderful opportunity for on-going skills development and education, learning about new and interesting programs, staying current on issues in the field, and connecting with colleagues from around the world.

ASSOCIATION FOR CONFLICT RESOLUTION *(a merged organization of Academy of Family Mediators, Society of Professionals in Dispute Resolution, and Conflict Resolution in Education Network)*
1527 New Hampshire Ave., NW
Washington, DC 20036
202-667-9700
www. acresolution.org

NATIONAL ASSOCIATION FOR COMMUNITY MEDIATION
1527 New Hampshire Ave., NW
Washington DC 20036
202-667-9700
www.mediate.com/nafcm

AMERICAN BAR ASSOCIATION SECTION OF DISPUTE RESOLUTION
740 15th Street NW
Washington, DC 20005
202-662-1680
www.abanet.org/dispute

AFCC: *an association of family court and community professionals*
6515 Grand Teton Plaza
Suite 210
Madison, WI 53719
608-664-3750
www.afccnet.org

CADRE: *Consortium for Appropriate Dispute Resolution in Special Education*
Direction Service
P.O. Box 51360
Eugene, OR 51360
541-686-5060
www.directionservice.org/cadre

JOURNALS & PUBLICATIONS

While many of the organizations above provide newsletters or other publications to members, here are some additional publications available by subscription.

CONCILIATION QUARTERLY
Mennonite Conciliation Service
21 S 12th Street
Box M
Akron, PA 17501
717-859-3889
mcs@mccus.org

CONFLICT RESOLUTION NOTES
204 37th Street
Suite 203
Pittsburgh, PA 15201
412-687-6210
www.ConflictRes.org

CONFLICT RESOLUTION QUARTERLY
Jossey-Bass Publishers
350 Sansome Street
San Francisco, CA 94104
888-378-2537
www.josseybass.com

OTHER RESOURCES

As the fields of mediation and conflict resolution have grown in popularity, so have the resources that are available. Here are some of my favorites.

NETWORK OF COMMUNITIES FOR PEACEMAKING & CONFLICT RESOLUTION
1718 East Speedway
Tucson, AZ 85719
520-670-1541
www.apeacemaker.net

Formerly the National Conference on Peacemaking and Conflict Resolution, this non-membership group organizes a large and diverse conference every two years and sponsors innovative programs.

MEDIATION INFORMATION AND RESOURCE CENTER
www.mediate.com

This web site is your link to resources, mediators, articles, organizations in the field, and more.

CONFLICT RESOLUTION CONSORTIUM
www.colorado.edu/conflict

Managed by Guy and Heidi Burgess at the University of Colorado, this site provides great insight into profound and intractable conflict and links to a variety of resources.

WOODBURY COLLEGE
660 Elm Street
Montpelier, VT
802-229-0516
www.woodbury-college.edu

Their year-long mediation and conflict resolution programs offer the best of academic programs and training courses without the commitment of a 4-year or 2-year course of traditional study nor the shortcomings of a 40-hour training.

BOOKS

There is an ever-growing bibliography of books on mediation, as well as ancillary topics such as negotiation, communication, and conflict resolution. Here are just a few that you may want to include on your shelf.

Beer, Jennifer, with Eileen Stief. *The Mediator's Handbook*, 3rd edition. Gabriola Island, BC: New Society Publishers, 1997.

Bush, Robert Baruch, and Joseph Folger. *The Promise of Mediation: Responding to Conflict Through Empowerment and Recognition*. San Francisco: Jossey-Bass, 1994.

Fisher, Robert, and William Ury. *Getting to Yes: Negotiating Agreement Without Giving In*, 2nd edition. NY: Penguin, 1991.

Folberg, Jay, and Alison Taylor. *Mediation: A Comprehensive Guide to Resolving Conflicts Without Litigation*. San Francisco: Jossey-Bass, 1984.

Folberg, Jay, and Ann Milne, eds. *Divorce Mediation: Theory and Practice*. New York: Guilford Press, 1988

Lang, Michael, and Alison Taylor. *The Making of a Mediator: Developing Artistry in Practice*. San Francisco: Jossey-Bass, 2000.

Mayer, Bernard. *The Dynamics of Conflict Resolution: A Practitioner's Guide*. San Francisco: Jossey-Bass, 2000.

Mennonite Conciliation Service. *Mediation and Facilitation Training Manual: Foundations and Skills for Constructive Conflict Transformation*, 4th edition. Akron, PA, 2000.

Moore, Christopher. *The Mediation Process: Practical Strategies for Resolving Conflict*, 2nd edition. San Francisco: Jossey-Bass, 1996.

Slaikeu, Karl. *When Push Comes to Shove: A Practical Guide to Mediating Disputes.* San Francisco: Jossey-Bass, 1996.

Yarbrough, Elaine, and William Wilmot. *Artful Mediation: Constructive Conflict at Work.* Boulder, CO: Cairns Publishing, 1995.

The End